God's
Little book of

Peace

Words of comfort and reassurance
RICHARD DALY

WILLIAM
COLLINS

William Collins
An Imprint of HarperCollins*Publishers*
77–85 Fulham Palace Road
London W6 8JB

www.williamcollinsbooks.com

1 3 5 7 9 10 8 6 4 2

First published in Great Britain in
2007 by HarperCollins*Publishers*
This edition 2013

© 2007 Richard Daly

Richard Daly asserts the moral right to be
identified as the author of this work

A catalogue record for this book is
available from the British Library

ISBN 978-0-00-752838-7

Printed and bound in China by
South China Printing Co. Ltd.

Introduction

In a world where distress and anxiety have become the norms, how can we truly experience peace in a peaceless world?

Harmony amongst nations and between people struck by terror and disaster is hard to come by. Yet in the midst of turmoil, peace can still be achieved. It is possible to live in a world without peace, and yet still be in peace. Such an experience comes only from knowing God.

This little volume is designed to provide you with insightful words to help you discover true peace for yourself.

Open this book at any page and
be inspired.

Richard Daly

Know God, know peace ...
no God, no peace

One of the many titles given to God is
'*Jehovah-Shalom*', which means 'the God of
Peace'. Our first step in finding true peace
is getting to know God.

For Further Reflection

Judges 6:24

Wish peace

The Jewish word for peace is *'shalom'*.
Its meaning signifies a deep inner wellbeing
that is often wished upon someone in
greeting. Greet someone today in this
way and wish peace into their life.

For Further Reflection
Daniel 4:1

Get connected

The greatest quest in life has always been
the search for peace. Many have travelled
far and wide, yet the path to peace is a direct
line between God and man ... the oneness
of divinity and humanity.

For Further Reflection
Jeremiah 29:13

Think tranquillity

Tranquillity – what a peaceful word.
Picture yourself in a tranquil scene –
by a calm flowing river, a serene sunset,
a quiet meadow. This in itself aids
peace of mind.

For Further Reflection
Philippians 4:7

Seek a peaceful remedy

It's not work that wears us out, but
worry, anxiety, stress, fear and everything
else that perplexes our minds. Inner peace
is the only antidote that banishes these
negative emotions.

For Further Reflection
Colossians 3:15

Pursue peace

Worry is something you permit; peace is something you pursue. That means you can learn to control what goes on in your mind.

For Further Reflection

John 14:7

Think peaceful thoughts

Agitation! Frustration! Complication! Just
the thought of these gives a sense of unrest.
Calm, tranquillity, serenity ... now doesn't
that just feel better?

For Further Reflection

Philippians 4:8

Clear your conscience

What greater peace of mind can be achieved than when you know you are doing God's will?

For Further Reflection

Isaiah 48:18
Ephesians 5:17

God is big!

To worry is to say to God, 'You're not big enough to solve this problem, so I'll deal with it myself'. Remember, you don't have a problem he can't solve.

For Further Reflection

Psalm 24:8
Psalm 121

Know your limits

Peace disappears when you try to do something about something you can't do anything about!

For Further Reflection

Matthew 19:26

Genesis 18:14

Delegate your worries

Ninety-two per cent of what we worry
about, we have no control over. Give the
other eight per cent to God and bask
in peace of mind.

For Further Reflection

Psalm 55:22
1 Peter 5:7

Kill overwork, not yourself

If you make your work more important
than yourself, you won't be around to
finish it.

For Further Reflection

Matthew 11:28–30
Romans 14:17

Live peace

'Let peace rule': that ought to
be your motto!

For Further Reflection

Colossians 3:15
Isaiah 55:12

Take a break

Never feel guilty about taking a break —
God didn't. Time taken in rest replenishes
your soul and aids a peaceful spirit.

For Further Reflection

Hebrews 4:3–5

Experience heaven in hell

When all hell is breaking loose around you,
yet you remain calm and confident, you're
experiencing the peace of God that
transcends all understanding.

For Further Reflection

Philippians 4:7

Just pray

Inner peace need not be all that elusive.
Just pray for it.

For Further Reflection

Philippians 4:6, 7
Jeremiah 29:7

Change your mind

Don't waste time focusing on things you can't change. Instead focus on things you can, like your perspective and attitude toward life.

For Further Reflection

Isaiah 26:3

Live for today

Live one peaceful day at a time. Remember,
yesterday is gone and tomorrow is unborn;
all you have is today.

For Further Reflection

Matthew 6:25
Matthew 6:11

Look to this day

Today well lived makes every yesterday
a dream of happiness and every tomorrow
a vision of hope.

For Further Reflection

Psalm 118:24
2 Corinthians 6:2

Work through your problems

Whatever problem is destroying your
peace, ask: What is the worst that can
possibly happen? Then prepare to accept
it, and peacefully proceed to improve
on the worst.

For Further Reflection

Romans 8:28, 31

Fear not

Fear is the opposite of peace.

For Further Reflection

1 John 4:18

Be rejuvenated

Peacefulness promotes the most relaxing
recreating forces – good health, good sleep,
laughter and happiness.

For Further Reflection

Isaiah 58:8

Seek wisdom in proverbs

'Don't cross your bridges before you come
to them' and 'don't cry over spilt milk' are two
old proverbs that can lead to a peaceful life.

For Further Reflection

Romans 12:16

Think peace, gain peace

Think miserable thoughts and be miserable.
Think fearful thoughts and be fearful.
Think peaceful thoughts and be peaceful.
You are what you think!

For Further Reflection

2 Corinthians 10:5
Proverbs 23:7

Don't hold grudges

To forgive is a powerful release of
pent-up feelings. It leads to freedom.
Freedom leads to peace.

For Further Reflection

2 Corinthians 2:7
Romans 12:17

Be grateful

Be grateful for what you have. A spirit of appreciation goes a long way to peaceful feelings.

For Further Reflection

Ephesians 5:20
Job 1:21
Hebrews 13:5

Count your blessings

It's not until something is taken away from you that you realise its importance. Count your blessings, not your troubles.

For Further Reflection

Ephesians 1:3
Hebrews 13:5

Turn your minus to plus

One of the traits of having a peaceful
character is the ability to turn unpleasant
experiences into positive lessons. Start
doing that today.

For Further Reflection

Jeremiah 31:13
Psalm 30:5

Be interested in others

In whatever problem you experience, there's always someone worse off than you. Discover other people's plights; it may make yours pale into insignificance.

For Further Reflection

Psalm 41:1
Proverbs 14:21
Galatians 6:2

Spread peace

Peace is contagious. Live peacefully and
it will rub off on people around you.

For Further Reflection
Isaiah 52:7–9

Seek reconciliation

When you are at peace with others, you will
ultimately be at peace with yourself.

For Further Reflection
Hebrews 12:14
Matthew 5:23–24

Tell God everything!

'Oh what peace we often forfeit,
Oh what needless pain we bear
All because we do not carry
Everything to God in prayer.'

Joseph Scriven

For Further Reflection
Matthew 7:7, 8
John 14:13, 4

Unburden your heart

Any psychiatrist will tell you it is therapeutic to share your problems. If you can't tell anyone trustworthy, you can always trust God.

For Further Reflection

Jeremiah 33:3
Isaiah 59:1

Reproduce peace

Peace begets peace. Each day ask
God to help you become an instrument
of his peace.

For Further Reflection

Nahum 1:15

Be still

The very word peace emits a sense of
stillness. Just being still long enough will
give you a vision of what peace can be.

For Further Reflection

Psalm 46:10

Be of one mind

Worry comes from the Greek word meaning
to 'divide the mind'. Peace counteracts that
and restores your mind to oneness.

For Further Reflection

Philippians 4:2
Luke 12:29–31

Speak truthfully

Honesty is still the best policy and leads
to inner contentment. Deception, falsity
and even half-truths will stifle your
search for peace.

For Further Reflection

John 8:32
Philippians 4:8

Relax

It has been clinically proven that any
nervous or emotional state fails to exist in
the presence of complete relaxation.
Make time to relax today.

For Further Reflection
Psalm 37:7–11

Take a power nap

Rest is not doing 'nothing'. Rest is repair.
A five-minute nap during the day will
help restore peaceful vitalities.

For Further Reflection

Mark 6:31–32

Hope

There are many people living with no hope.
Hope gives you purpose and direction;
it is the oil that fuels peace.

For Further Reflection

Romans 15:13

Seek forgiveness

Ultimate peace begins when we have
peace with God. Regardless of your past,
he is willing to forgive and forget.
Just ask him.

For Further Reflection

Romans 5:1
1 John 1:9

Appreciate yourself

Peace is also dependent on how we feel about ourselves. A routine of exercise generates a feel good factor.

For Further Reflection
Ephesians 5:29

Eat healthily

Are you eating properly? If you aren't,
it will affect your energy levels, your
moods and hence your peace.

For Further Reflection

1 Corinthians 6:19, 20
Ephesians 5:29

Pace yourself

Stress wears down your immune system
and makes you vulnerable to the very
things you fear.

For Further Reflection
Proverbs 19:2

Trust in God

Trust is the highest form of faith because
it doesn't need to know all the answers ...
trust God and let peace take over.

For Further Reflection

Proverbs 3:5–6
2 Samuel 22:3

Be content

It is better to be content with little than anxious having too much. Peace is not about what or who you are, but how you are.

For Further Reflection

Luke 3:14

Just say no

The demands of life can be overwhelming.
In order for peace to flourish, learn to say 'no'.

For Further Reflection
Galatians 5:22, 23

Accept his love

No matter how unworthy you feel today,
nothing can shut off God's flowing
love for you.

For Further Reflection

Songs of Solomon 8:7
John 3:16

Believe God!

God's opinion of you, and his opinion alone,
is the only reliable basis on which to build
your self-worth. Never forget that!

For Further Reflection

Isaiah 43:1, 2
Psalm 139 1–24

Relax your muscles

Right now, unless your entire body is as limp as an old rag doll, you are at this very moment producing nervous and muscular tensions. Relax, relax, relax.

For Further Reflection

Psalm 46:10

Make peace a habit

Tension is a habit. Relaxing is a habit.
Bad habits can be broken, good habits
can be developed.

For Further Reflection
Ephesians 5:15

Avoid a 'must do' attitude

What limits peace? A sense of 'must' or
'obligation'; the unending list of things ahead
that simply have to be done!

For Further Reflection

Ecclesiastes 3:1–9

Read Psalm 23

Psalm 23 provides a wonderful picture of tranquillity and peace: 'He leads me to lie down in green pastures, he leads me beside still waters, he restores my soul.'

For Further Reflection

Psalm 23

Let others judge

You will instinctively know if you are in a
state of peacefulness and those around you
will know, too ... including your dog!

For Further Reflection
Matthew 5:16

Let God heal

Broken relationships can often lead to broken hearts. God promises to heal the broken-hearted. Not only does he heal, he also restores.

For Further Reflection

Psalm 147:3
Psalm 145:14, 15
Jeremiah 30:17

Forgive others

Forgiving others not only releases you, it frees the offender. Both of you can then move on in life.

For Further Reflection

Mark 9:50

Make peaceful choices

Major decisions in life often cause anxiety.
Avoid it by taking time to pray and seek
godly counsel before you proceed.

For Further Reflection
Jeremiah 29:11–13

Be a mediator

Mediation involves being a 'go-between'
for two people in need. It is the ultimate
way to become a peacemaker.

For Further Reflection

Matthew 5:9
Ephesians 4:2–4

Embrace God's peace

World peace is very much an illusion.
But with the peace of God, you can live
peacefully in a peaceless world.

For Further Reflection

John 14:27

Go somewhere peaceful

To evoke peace go to a place of peace:
a quiet garden; beside a babbling brook – any
place where your soul can be uplifted.

For Further Reflection

Isaiah 32:18
1 Timothy 2:2

Wish peace to others

Keep praying for peace in war-torn countries.
Your prayers could be their only hope.

For Further Reflection
Luke 10:5

Spirituality leads to peace

The Bible counsels that to have our minds
'on the world' leads to death, but to be
spiritually-minded leads to peace and life.

For Further Reflection

Romans 8:6

Slow down

The tempo of modern life is not conducive to rest and relaxation. Slow down! There's no one winner in the race of life.

For Further Reflection

1 Corinthians 9:24–27

Hold on

When you're at your lowest point and everything you've tried has failed, don't throw in the towel – you may be closer to a breakthrough than what you think!

For Further Reflection

Isaiah 54:17

Actualise

Talk peaceful to be peaceful.

For Further Reflection

Colossians 4:6

Leave it to God

What you can't accomplish by worrying
all night, God can accomplish in an instant
by his spoken word.

For Further Reflection
Psalm 46:6, 7

Live peaceably

There is calmness when life is lived
in gratitude and quiet joy.

For Further Reflection
Psalm 107:29, 30

Speak peacefully

Your words are like nitro-glycerine: they
can either blow up bridges or heal hearts.
Be careful what you say; in your tongue
lays the power for life or death.

For Further Reflection

Romans 12:18
Isaiah 50:4–7

Don't lose your peace

Next time you get all worked up, ask yourself:
What is the enemy trying to do?
His plan is to steal your joy.

For Further Reflection

Exodus 14:14
Job 13:5

Control your thoughts

Direct your thoughts to those virtues
that inspire you – hope, joy, love
and thankfulness.

For Further Reflection
Jeremiah 29:11
Luke 24:38, 39

Bitter to sweetness

Betrayal is something others do to you.
Bitterness is something you develop yourself!
Look past the hurt and you'll see that
your resentment is just a roadblock to
your own peace.

For Further Reflection

Ephesians 4:31
Hebrews 12:15

Guard your mind!

We are encouraged to 'take captive every thought and make it obedient to Christ'. When we actively police our minds, our defence will begin to grow strong.

For Further Reflection

2 Corinthians 5:10

Be at peace with yourself

When you withhold forgiveness you hurt
yourself more – much more! It hangs
over you like a cloud, affecting everything
you do. Forgiveness releases peace and
restoration. So forgive today!

For Further Reflection

Matthew 6:12
1 Kings 8:50

Love in action

All genuine works of love are works
of peace. So keep loving.

For Further Reflection
Matthew 5:44
Luke 6:35

Be honest

If you always tell the truth, you never have
to worry about remembering what you said.
Nothing is more important that credibility.
Lose that and you can lose everything.

For Further Reflection

Romans 12:17

Smile awhile

Peace starts with a smile. It's as simple as that!

For Further Reflection

Numbers 6:26

Encourage someone today

One basic human need is to be appreciated.
We all think wonderful things about people
but never tell them. Praise becomes valuable
only when you impart it. Tell someone today
how much you appreciate them.

For Further Reflection

Romans 12:6–8

Peace begets peace

The peace of God enables us to live in peace with God, with ourselves and with our fellow man.

For Further Reflection
Romans 5:1

Just listen

One word from God – just one word –
can change everything for you. Take time
out to listen for that word today.

For Further Reflection
Ezekiel 4:7
2 Kings 20:16

Let God lead

When you surrender to Christ, you look
at life through his eyes. This enables you
to handle life through his strength.

For Further Reflection

John 14:16

Sleep well!

Sleep is a gift from God. The Psalmist says:
It is vain to sit up late ... for so he gives up
his beloved sleep. Maybe the most spiritual
thing you can do right now is put this
book down and take a nap!

For Further Reflection

Psalm 127:2
Ecclesiastes 5:12

Love one another

Anything that makes it difficult to love our
fellow man makes it difficult to love God.

For Further Reflection

John 13:34
1 John 4:7

Don't leave out God

Don't get so involved in the work of God
that you neglect the God of the work!

For Further Reflection

John 15:5

A comfort thought

The Holy Spirit is our comforter.
Isn't that comforting to know?

For Further Reflection

John 14:16
John 14:26

Pray

When in need, pray this prayer:
Prince of peace I need you. Take charge.
I need comfort and courage that comes
from your Spirit. Let me find you in a quiet
place where I can hear your heartbeat
and feel secure. Amen.

For Further Reflection
Psalm 62:8

Let peace flow

When the Holy Spirit fills your life,
you immediately become a channel
of God's love and his peace.

For Further Reflection
Psalm 37:11

Control yourself

'Self' will always find reasons to be
dissatisfied. Your spirit will always search
for reasons to be thankful. Both are at
enmity; the winner depends on you.
Let your spirit rule.

For Further Reflection
1 Thessalonians 5:18

Learn from others

Read the scriptures and see how often
the peace of God sustained and carried
people through, even Jesus Christ.

For Further Reflection
John 5:39

Trust in God

By maintaining your peace when under attack, you're telling the Devil, 'I'm still trusting in God'. This baffles the enemy.

For Further Reflection

Ephesians 6:13

Seek reconciliation

Jesus said: When you offer your gift at the altar, and you remember that someone has something against you, leave your gift and go and make peace first. It's still the best advice for reconciliation.

For Further Reflection
Matthew 5:23, 24

Amazing grace

Never underestimate the glorious gift of grace. Jesus gave his life for you and wishes to grant you complete restoration.

For Further Reflection

Ephesians 2:8

Perfect love

Whatever your circumstances, always
remember that God loves you with an
unfathomable love that cannot be measured,
and that is totally perfect.

For Further Reflection

Jeremiah 31:3
Nahum 1:7

He that is greater

Remember there is One greater than you,
in whom all fear dissolves.

For Further Reflection
1 John 4:4

Gain everlasting peace

Jesus is the same yesterday, today and forever. This means the peace he offers is timeless.

For Further Reflection
Hebrews 13:8

Claim God's gift

Peace is the gift of God.

For Further Reflection

1 John 4:18
2 Timothy 1:7

Avoid doubt

It will surprise you how often the thing you
fear the most will never come to pass.

For Further Reflection

Deuteronomy 1:21
Matthew 21:21

Gratitude

Having a spirit of gratitude is like a tonic:
it smoothes the ruffled brow and places a
smile upon the countenance.

For Further Reflection

1 Samuel 12:24
Psalm 126:3

Multiply your blessings

There are two ways to multiply our blessings.
One is to recognise them, the other is to
share them.

For Further Reflection
Ephesians 1:3

Rest

The way of escape that God offers us is not a flight, but a release. He says: 'Come unto me and I will give you rest.'

For Further Reflection

Matthew 11:28
Exodus 20:8–11

Be free in Christ

When you know your sins are truly forgiven,
you know you are truly free.

For Further Reflection
Galatians 5:1

Leave it with God

Having turned your problem over to God,
cease worrying and go peacefully about
other duties. It is no longer your matter,
but his.

For Further Reflection
Psalm 55:22

The future is bright with God

Worry is blind and cannot discern the future,
but God sees the end from the beginning.

For Further Reflection
Revelation 1:8

Spread love

If feeling despondent, visit someone not as fortunate as you. Pass on a cheery word of comfort. I guarantee you will feel lifted too.

For Further Reflection
Galatians 6:2

Use your imagination

We are told worry is what continues after a danger is passed or before it arrives. It thrives on imagination. Therefore fill your mind with peaceful thoughts so there's no room for anything else.

For Further Reflection

Isaiah 26:3

Enjoy today

The future is today. Live for today, enjoy today – it comes but only once.

For Further Reflection

Psalm 118:24

Swap bad for good

Suppression is not a good way to deal with bad feelings. Substitution is better. Rid yourself of them by transferring them with encouraging thoughts concerning God.

For Further Reflection

Ezekiel 18:31

Seek peace

Follow after the things that make for peace ...
things that are true, honest and just.

For Further Reflection

Philippians 4:8
Romans 14:19

Turn smiles into laughter

The ability to make someone laugh is a rare
creative gift, yet it only begins with a smile.

For Further Reflection
Psalm 126:2
Proverbs 15:13

Express yourself

Writing out your troubled thoughts on paper
extracts the mind of haphazard thinking. Try
doing this and experience a mental release.

For Further Reflection

Jeremiah 30:2
1 John 1:4
Revelation 1:19

Be creative

'A picture paints a thousand words'.
Try expressing yourself through painting
– it's a healing balm.

For Further Reflection
Philippians 4:7

Breathe in, breathe out

Deep rhythmic breathing is a splendid aid
to relaxation. It improves circulation, frees
the lungs, stimulates the brain, steadies the
nerves and gives a feeling of control and
poise. Try it right now.

For Further Reflection

3 John 2

Affirm someone

Affirmations motivate us to move forward.
Try affirming someone today by giving
a genuine word of approval.

For Further Reflection
Philippians 2:3

Be content

Learn to be content with what you have:
a quiet home; a few books of inspiration;
a few trustworthy friends; and a hundred
innocent pleasures that bring no pain
or remorse.

For Further Reflection
1 Timothy 6:8

Be childlike

Children have no thought for the past
or the future. They enjoy the moment.
Follow them into their beautiful and
enchanting world.

For Further Reflection

Matthew 19:14
Psalm 127:3

Find solitude

Solitude is much more than the mere
absence of noise or cessation of movement.
In the midst of turmoil, you can have
stillness in the secret refuge of your soul.

For Further Reflection

Psalm 23
Psalm 72:3

Get a soul mate

When you come across a kindred spirit who
sees you 'eye to eye', regard the meeting
as having been brought by providence and
enjoy a new friendship. It was meant to be.

For Further Reflection
Proverbs 27:9

Avoid gloomy people!

People who have gloomy moods attract
to themselves gloomy people and gloomy
people have a knack of producing gloomy
situations. Avoid them!

For Further Reflection

Proverbs 15:12, 18
Proverbs 22:24–25

Look for the good

When misfortunes arise, consider that it
may be a blessing in disguise.

For Further Reflection

Deuteronomy 28:2
Ephesians 1:3

Angel delight

In times of need, remember that God
sends his angels to camp around those
who trust him, and to deliver them
from their troubles.

For Further Reflection

Psalm 34:7

Inspire yourself

In times of ailment very often the body will heal itself, especially when you feed the mind with words such as 'Be strong and of a good courage.'

For Further Reflection
Joshua 1:9

Questions, questions

Serenity. Three phrases you should let go
from your mind if you want to be serene
are 'what if?', 'if only' and 'why me?'

For Further Reflection

Proverbs 3:5, 6

Accept the best

You can't have the best of everything,
but you can make the best of what
you've got.

Reach for the sky

Your thoughts set the limits of your actions.
If you aim for the highest you may not reach
it, but the spot at which you do arrive may
not be far off the mark.

For Further Reflection

Proverbs 23:7

Medicine for life

Our rations of adversities are really medicines
prescribed by the Great Physician for our
ultimate benefit. Each dose contains
ingredients for eternal life.

For Further Reflection
Job 23:10

Get over it!

No anxiety lasts forever or even for very
long. Whatever you are going through,
it, too, shall pass.

For Further Reflection

1 Peter 5:7

Respect yourself, respect others

'Do unto others as you would want them do to you'. This is the golden rule of peace.

For Further Reflection

Luke 6:31

Stay calm

Many aches and pains are of emotional
origin. Back pain, excessive perspiration,
palpitations and ulcers: all have their root
in negative emotion. Next time you feel
discomfort, check your mood.

For Further Reflection

Psalm 25:18
Job 15:20
Daniel 5:6

Appreciate yourself

Note the things you are good at and
concentrate your efforts on them. Remind
yourself from time to time of your
worthwhile qualities. There's nothing
wrong with self-praise.

For Further Reflection

Psalm 139:14

First things first

The best anti-stress device is to start your
day with prayer and meditation.

For Further Reflection

Mark 1:35

Keep your friends

Take time off for friendship. Your quality of
life can be greatly enriched by maintaining
those special ties. So will theirs.

For Further Reflection

Proverbs 17:17

The best medicine

Laughter will lower your blood pressure, keep
ulcers at bay, reduce your worries, tone up
your nervous system and above all make
your face more pleasant to look at!

For Further Reflection

Proverbs 17:22
Proverbs 15:13

Pray for daily bread

For each new day, pray for enough
strength for that day, enough love for that
day, enough hope for that day, enough
peace for that day.

For Further Reflection

Psalm 29:11

Keep your mind clean

The human mind is the most powerful
healing force in the world, not matched
by any drug. Avoid contamination by
impure thoughts!

For Further Reflection

Jeremiah 4:14

Help someone

However insignificant, try to make time
for one small act of service each day.

For Further Reflection

Ephesians 4:32

A hug a day

Hugging is remedial. It ceases depression
and reduces stress. It has no unpleasant side
effects and is nothing less than a miracle
drug. Give someone a hug today!

For Further Reflection

Songs 8:3

Think positive

We can think of only one thought at any given time. Invariably one kind of thought is driven out by another. You can learn to dispel negative thinking by simply replacing them with positive ones.

For Further Reflection

Philippians 2:6

Surrender

If you need reconciliation after a
disagreement with someone, try giving
a peace offering. It's a sure way of
starting a truce.

For Further Reflection

Proverbs 7:14

Meditate

'Whatsoever things are true, whatsoever
things are lovely, and whatsoever things
are honest, think on these things.'

For Further Reflection

Philippians 4:8

Watch out!

God has more for you! You haven't
seen your best days yet. There's more
ahead than behind you. So be prepared
for exciting things.

For Further Reflection

Isaiah 43:18–19

Cast your cares

'Be anxious for nothing'. All it does is
distort your mind.

For Further Reflection

1 Peter 5:7

Showers of blessing

To the stormy winds and waves Jesus said,
'Peace be still', and there was a great calm.
He can do the same in your storms of life.

For Further Reflection
Mark 4:39

Be made whole

God's plan is not simply to repair your
brokenness; it is to make you a new creature.
That's why He's been revealing, removing
and restoring certain things in your life.

For Further Reflection

2 Corinthians 5:17
Galatians 4:19

Be an overcomer

Jesus said: In this world you will have tribulations, but be of good cheer, I have overcome the world.

For Further Reflection

John 16:33

Be a peacemaker

Blessed are the peacemakers, for they
shall be called God's children.

For Further Reflection

Matthew 5:9

It's God's way, not yours

In difficult times, God teaches us that despite
our knowledge, skills and experience to solve
problems, we only ultimately overcome 'not
by might, nor by power, but by my spirit'.

For Further Reflection
Zechariah 4:6

Peace in crisis

Guard your inward peace, even if your
whole world is in turmoil.

For Further Reflection

Psalm 112:6
Psalm 122:7, 8

Freely accept

Peace is one of the fruits of the Spirit.
It is the evidence of a spirit-filled life. The
good news is that God's Spirit is free to all.

For Further Reflection

Galatians 5:22

Self-analysis

What's blocking you from experiencing
God's joy? Find out as soon as you can
and refuse to live another day with it.

For Further Reflection

Nehemiah 8:10

Live God's will

When you know you're doing God's will,
you experience a lasting pleasure that
simply can't be found anywhere else!

For Further Reflection
Matthew 7:21

Love your neighbour

Lets face it; sometimes confrontation does end in permanent division. That's why 'if possible, live peaceably with all men'.

For Further Reflection
Romans 12:18

Look for the good in others

Compliments by their very nature are
biodegradable, and tend to dissolve hours
or days after we receive them; that is
why we can always use another.

For Further Reflection

Ephesians 4:25
Ephesians 6:8

Be an intercessor

When God prompts you to pray for someone else, don't wait. Do it! Your prayers may be the only one thing standing between that person and catastrophe.

For Further Reflection

2 Thessalonians 3:1

Admit your faults

One step toward recovering your peace
is to admit that you are creating most
of your stress.

For Further Reflection

Psalm 32:5
1 John 1:9

Pray without ceasing

Heaven stops to listen to your prayer.
Think about that! Your thoughts, struggles
and goals may not mean much to others,
but they register with God.

For Further Reflection

1 Thessalonians 5:17

Turn stones to steps

Some people grow through failure, while
others never recover from it. What is the
difference? See your mistakes as stepping-
stones rather than stumbling blocks.

For Further Reflection

Psalm 130:4

Be teachable

If you are facing a problem right now,
ask: Lord what do you want me to learn
from this? Then trust God and grow
stronger through it.

For Further Reflection
Psalm 23:6